Sports

I Can Bowl

By Edana Eckart

Welcome Books

Children's Press®
A Division of Scholastic Inc.
New York / Toronto / London / Auckland / Sydney
Mexico City / New Delhi / Hong Kong
Danbury, Connecticut

Photo Credits: Cover and all photos by Maura B. McConnell
Contributing Editor: Jennifer Silate
Book Design: Christopher Logan

Library of Congress Cataloging-in-Publication Data

Eckart, Edana.
I can bowl / by Edana Eckart.
      p. cm. — (Sports)
   Includes bibliographical references (p.) and index.
   Summary: When a young girl and her father go bowling, she shows how to play the game.
      ISBN 0-516-23972-4 (lib. bdg.) — ISBN 0-516-24028-5 (pbk.)
      1. Bowling—Juvenile literature. [1. Bowling.] I. Title.

GV903. 5 .E35 2002
794.6—dc21

                                                            2001058112

Contents

1 Going Bowling 4

2 Bowling Shoes 6

3 Knocking Down Pins 10

4 New Words 22

5 To Find Out More 23

6 Index 24

7 About the Author 24

My name is Emma.

Today, Dad and I are going **bowling**.

We must wear **special** shoes to bowl.

They will not **scratch** the wooden floor.

My shoes are red, white, and blue.

7

I choose the **bowling ball** that I will use.

The bowling ball is heavy.

There are ten **pins** at the end of the **lane**.

I roll the bowling ball at the pins.

I try to **knock** them down.

I knocked down six pins!

I have to knock down
four more.

Now, I will try to knock down the rest of the pins.

I roll the bowling ball again.

15

I knocked them down!

Now, it is Dad's turn to bowl.

Dad rolls his bowling ball at the pins.

He rolls the ball hard!

19

Dad knocked down all of the pins!

Dad and I are good bowlers.

Bowling is fun.

21

New Words

bowling (**boh**-ling) a game played by rolling a heavy ball down a lane at wooden pins

bowling ball (**boh**-ling **bawl**) a heavy ball used to knock down pins when bowling

knock (**nok**) to hit and cause to fall down

lane (**layn**) a narrow wooden path on which bowling balls are rolled

pins (**pinz**) bottle-shaped pieces of wood or plastic that are knocked down in bowling

scratch (**skrach**) to make a mark or cut

special (**spesh**-uhl) different or unusual

22

To Find Out More

Books

Bowling for Beginners: Simple Steps to Strikes & Spares
by Don Nace
Sterling Publications

Web Site
Bowl.com - Fun & Games
http://www.bowl.com/templates/BowlDotCom/common/fun/index.html
Play fun online games, send bowling e-cards to your friends, and learn all about bowling on this Web site.

Brunswickids E-Club
http://www.brunswickids.com/
Play online bowling games, find a bowling center near you, and much more on this fun Web site.

Index

bowling, 4, 20   lane, 10   shoes, 6

bowling ball,
   8, 10, 14, 18 pins, 10, 12,
                14, 18, 20

About the Author

Edana Eckart has written several children's books. She enjoys bike riding with her family.

Reading Consultants

Kris Flynn, Coordinator, Small School District Literacy, The San Diego County Office of Education

Shelly Forys, Certified Reading Recovery Specialist, W.J. Zahnow Elementary School, Waterloo, IL

Sue McAdams, Former President of the North Texas Reading Council of the IRA, and Early Literacy Consultant, Dallas, TX